The National Teaching & Advisory Service

A Foster Carers' Guide To Education

Written by Barry Dixon

Published by The National Teaching & Advisory Service
© No part of this publication may be reproduced, stored in a retrieval system or transmitted in any form or by any means, electronic, mechanical, photocopying, recording or otherwise, without the prior permission of the publisher.

ISBN 978-09547627-6-6

Published Sept 2012.

Foreword

It is now over three decades since we were made aware of the extent to which children in public care so scandalously underachieve in the education system. For all the undeniable progress that has been made, the gap in performance between looked after children and those within the general school population is still monumental, and totally unacceptable. It is widely accepted that this failure has little to do with children's backgrounds, abilities or aspirations, and has more to do with the structure and operation of a care system that has proved largely resistant to change.

> The education of children in public care is about much more than academic performance alone. Successful participation in mainstream schools for children who are fostered enhances the stability of their home lives and provides an important context in which many who will have endured appallingly traumatic experiences may begin – sometimes for the first time – to experience a 'normal' life. Schools also provide important opportunities for personal and social development, and facilitate genuine participation and inclusion within neighbourhoods. We know, too, that successful education is the most reliable of all possible routes out of poverty, alienation and despair.

The significance and contribution of foster carers cannot be exaggerated. These are special people who give much within their personal lives to give children life chances that others simply take for granted. They deserve and should expect as much support as any of us are able to provide. This should include high levels of education support that for the overwhelming majority of children remains either non-existent or tokenistic. It is not surprising that education achievements for fostered children are still scandalously low.

This updated education guidance for foster carers is designed to help them weave their way through an education system that is complex, ever-changing and now bears little resemblance to our own school experiences. This latest edition incorporates the most recent educational developments and provides a greater range of information than we have previously published. It can never be more than a modest contribution to raising standards of education for children living with foster carers. We still have a long journey ahead before these highly vulnerable children get anything that remotely resembles a fair and equal chance in life. As ever the adults continue to hold the key to what is possible.

Tim Walker

Chief Executive - The National Teaching & Advisory Service
Director of Three Circles Fostering

CONTENTS

FOREWORD	1
INTRODUCTION	3
1. ADMISSIONS	5
2. TYPES OF SCHOOL	7
3. FURTHER EDUCATION	13
4. THE NATIONAL CURRICULUM	16
5. TEACHING METHODS	17
6. WHAT IS A KEY STAGE?	18
7. EXAMS AND TESTING	20
8. EXAM REVISION	22
9. TRANSITION	24
10. HOME-SCHOOL AGREEMENTS	29
11. GOVERNING BODIES	36
12. SPECIAL EDUCATIONAL NEEDS	37
13. INCLUSION	41
14. WHO DO I NEED TO KNOW?	43
15. COMMUNICATIONS	46
16. PUPIL RECORDS	48
17. PARENT TEACHER INTERVIEWS	50
18. EXCLUSION	53
19. EDUCATIONAL VISITS OR TRIPS	55
20. CHILD EMPLOYMENT	57
21 SOCIAL NETWORKING-SHOULD I BE WORRIED?	59
22. HOW TO COMPLAIN	61
23. TOP TWENTY TIPS FOR CARERS	64
GLOSSARY OF TERMS	65

INTRODUCTION

2012 is proving to be a year when apart from world recession, a European crisis and continued conflicts around the globe, our education system is facing dramatic and rapid change. There are so many new proposals and initiatives that it would even be difficult for education experts to keep up with events. It is therefore particularly important that those with responsibility for children in public care are kept well informed about these developments. Looked After Children still continue to perform badly in the school system, usually through no fault of their own. Nearly every survey shows that they massively underachieve at each stage of education and this may cause huge problems for the rest of their lives. In 2011 there were 65,000 Looked After Children in England alone, and nearly 30% of these vulnerable young people left school with no formal educational qualifications. If there is to be any major improvement then everybody working with these young people has to be prepared to give support and help. This handbook is designed to help you become involved with schools and the staff in them, so that together you can make a difference.

> There is widespread agreement that while children in public care are no more or less able than the general population, their educational success is extremely poor. Although outcomes for children in care have improved, recent statistics (2011) show that these children:

- Are seven times more likely to be excluded from school
- Perform badly at Key Stage tests compared with other pupils
- Are nine times more likely to have a statement of Special Educational Needs
- Perform badly at GCSE, where only 70% gained one GCSE, or similar qualification, compared with more than 99% of their age group, and 12% achieved 5 A*-C at GCSE, compared with 65% of other students
- Rarely attend university. Only 6% entered Higher Education in 2010 compared with 40% nationally
- Often leave school without any qualifications. In 2011 33% of young people in care were classified as NEET (Not in Education, Employment or Training) at the age of 19.

The education system is often extremely difficult to find your way around. The introduction of Free Schools and a huge rise in the number of Academies (see Section 2) has made it even more complicated and it's easy to lose the will to battle through the jargon and professional language which creates such a barrier between schools and users. It is tempting to leave it to the "professionals" but evidence shows that the more you know about the system the more likely you are to be able to support children in your care. There has been a much greater focus recently on children in care, particularly since the publication of various reports, starting with a Government paper in 2003 called "Every Child Matters." (See **www.everychildmatters.gov.uk/**). The aim of this development was to give every child, whatever their background or circumstances, the support they need. Although this is no longer Coalition Government policy the basic principles still form an important basis for our approach to education and care.

> The first thing to remember is that help is available and at various points in this guide you will be advised who to turn to when events or situations become difficult or confusing. It isn't necessary to understand every detail of how schools work, but it is important that you have enough information about them, to allow you to feel comfortable when speaking with teachers working with the young people in your care. Each section of this handbook will give some detail about a particular topic such as examinations, admissions to schools or questions to ask at parents' evenings. Links such as web sites and general contacts are provided, where appropriate, so that you can research the subject more thoroughly should the need arise.

1. ADMISSIONS.

Every child of compulsory school age, which is from the beginning of the term following the child's fifth birthday until the last Friday in June of year 11, has the right to a free school place provided by the Local Authority (LA). The LA must by law offer a child a place in a local school, but many schools are oversubscribed and are unable to accommodate all the children who would like to attend. Those with parental responsibility have the right to express a preference relating to choice of school, and the Government is increasing those choices, but that does not guarantee a place at your first choice school. If the application is not successful an appeal can be made to an independent panel that will consider the case. The appeal process will be explained in a letter from the Local Authority when they write to inform the parent or legal guardian that their application for a place has been unsuccessful. The letter should also contain a deadline date by which an appeal must be made. Under the Schools Admissions Code (2012) children in care must be given the highest priority when applying for school places even if the school is oversubscribed.

> Parents, or those with parental responsibility, have a duty to ensure that their child receives education between the ages of 5 and 16. It is, however, permissible for older children, usually 14-16 year olds, to be educated off site at a college or workplace, and there are increasing demands for this option to be used more widely. Normally this works on a day release basis, but with the introduction of work related courses (see sections 3 & 7) it has become more popular as another way of tackling disaffection and boredom at the beginning of the 14-19 phase of education.

Many authorities now admit children to primary schools at the beginning of the term during which the child becomes five, but you don't have to send your child to school before they are five. Because schools are now also admitting pupils well before the age of five, the preferred choice of school must be researched well in advance and it is advisable to apply early. Find out who deals with the admissions; is it the school or the Local Authority? Transfer to secondary school is slightly easier because the young person is already in the system but a decision still has to be made about which secondary school they will attend.

It is permissible for independent schools and state grammar schools to select pupils by ability. Specialist secondary schools can select up to 10% of their pupils who demonstrate a talent for their area of specialism, e.g. sports or languages (see section 2). Applications are normally made to secondary schools around September-November in the year before a child is due to start there. Transfer to post-16 education needs just as much investigation and should start in the 10th year nearly two years before sixth form studies begin. (see sections 3 and 9).

Before applying for a place:

- Check out your local schools. Be aware that if you live some distance away from the school you may have to appeal to an independent panel to get a place for the child in your care

- Visit the school, with the child

- Try and see the school on a normal working day

- Talk with other parents about their experiences

- Collect any school booklets or handbooks, which should give a clear picture not only of its admissions policy but also what the school can offer the child socially, emotionally and academically

- Pick up Local Authority documentation, which will probably give information about all schools in your area and their admission policies. Academies and Free Schools will provide their own information

- Look at performance or league tables produced by the Department for Education (DFE)

- Consult any Ofsted inspection reports on the school

- Ensure that the school can appropriately meet the physical and emotional needs of the young person

- Consider practical arrangements such as distance from home and convenience of public transport.

2. TYPES OF SCHOOL.

The school your child will attend depends mainly on their age and where you live, but can also be affected by religion, health and sometimes gender, in addition to any special educational requirements that the child might have. You have the right to be involved in choosing which school you believe will best meet the needs of the young person in your care, together with those who have parental responsibility, but you are not guaranteed a place. However, the Schools Admissions Code of 2012 should help to ensure that children in public care are given top priority when applying for places in local schools. If teachers from our own organisation, the National Teaching and Advisory Service are involved, they will regard organising a suitable school placement as a major part of their responsibility. So what sort of educational experience can you expect for your child?

PRE-SCHOOL EDUCATION

- Is mostly for children between the ages of two and five and is not compulsory
- Covers playgroups, child minders, voluntary and private nurseries as well as state run nurseries, which are all now inspected by The Office for Standards in Education (Ofsted)
- Playgroups mainly work with children between the ages of three and five but a large number do admit children below the age of three
- Nursery classes in state primary schools also take children from the age of three and, like playgroups, normally offer five half-day sessions a week in term time
- Private nursery schools take children between the ages of two and five and many stay open during school holidays
- Day nurseries can be run by local authorities or voluntary/private organizations and often cater for very young children. They are open for the whole working day and children attend according to their needs
- Child minders look after pre-school children and older children, after school and in the holidays. Child minders register as part of a network to provide early years education. Registered child minders are inspected by Ofsted to ensure national standards in terms of safety, opportunities for learning and play and the suitability of the environment. A registered child minder must be police checked and undertake an introductory child minding course
- The Government has now fulfilled a pledge to offer free part-time nursery places for all three and four year olds. They are entitled to 15 hours per week for 38 weeks of the year.

It is also worth mentioning Sure Start in this section, which is a Government programme set up to improve prospects for children and families, especially those living in disadvantaged situations. It aims to increase and improve childcare for these families but also focuses on the health and well being of the children before they start school. Support is offered to parents who are seeking employment, and financial advice is also available. Sure Start programmes are aimed at parents expecting a child as well as those with children up to the age of five. Although many Sure Start centres have been threatened with closure because of budget cuts in 2012, vigorous local campaigns have been successful in persuading many local politicians that they are too vital a resource to lose.

PRIMARY SCHOOLS

- Primary education begins at the age of five
- The first year of primary is reception and the second year is called year 1 for the purposes of the National Curriculum (see section 4)
- It is quite common for children to go to school at the start of the term before they are five
- Most schools take pupils at just one point in the year, normally September, which means that some summer born children start school very shortly after their fourth birthdays
- Children in the reception class may start with half-day attendance, which gradually builds up to full-time
- A primary school usually has an infant department (5-7 years - Key Stage 1) and a junior department (7-11 years- Key Stage 2) (see section 6)
- In some parts of England e.g. Dorset or Harrow, schools take 5-8 year olds as the first stage of a three-part system: first, middle (9-13 year olds) and upper (14-16 year olds).

SECONDARY SCHOOLS

These are schools for 11-16 year olds or 11-18 year olds depending on the way the education is organised in your locality. This has become a very complicated area in the last few years with Governments arguing that there needs to be a number of different types of secondary school to meet the needs of individual children. Find out what is happening locally. Does your preferred school cover the whole 11-18 age group, which means it will have a sixth form? Is it an 11-16 school with children moving to sixth form colleges for further study? Are there Academies and/or Free Schools? Is there a grammar school system? If there is, there will be an exam during Year 6 of primary school, which will decide what sort of secondary school your child will attend. If you would like further information about the way children transfer from primary to secondary, see section 9.

There are four main types of state secondary school:

1. Community schools are local high schools, which most children attend and are controlled by the Local Authority. You might just think of these as your neighbourhood comprehensive

2. Foundation and Trust schools are also run by the Local Authority but the governing body is the employer, which can set its own criteria for admitting children

3. Voluntary-aided schools are usually owned by charitable bodies, for example the church, but maintained by Local Authorities. These schools have to provide some money towards their running costs but can also set their own criteria for admission

4. Voluntary-controlled schools are owned by charitable organisations but the local authority employs staff, maintains buildings and sets admission policies.

New types of school have emerged in recent years as additions to the list. City Technology Colleges (CTC) have been around for a while now and as the name suggests they specialise in Information Technology. Academies are even more recent and are growing rapidly in number. By 2011 there were 629 Academies in place and by the end of 2012 it is expected there will be over 3000. The Department for Education (DfE) describes both CTCs and Academies as, "Publicly funded independent schools." They are often sponsored by large organisations or businesses and are allowed to operate in a slightly different way to normal mainstream secondary schools. However there is an even newer initiative - Free Schools. The law allowing them to set up was introduced in 2011. These will be run by, amongst others, groups of interested parents, teachers, charities, businesses, universities and religious or voluntary bodies but they are not allowed to make a profit. They will be funded directly from central government and just like Academies are totally free from Local Authority control.

> In most cases how the school is organised will have no effect on the quality of education it delivers, but it may become important if for example the birth parents have strong personal preferences. .

PRIVATE/INDEPENDENT SCHOOLS

These schools are registered with the Department for Education and are inspected but do not have to teach the National Curriculum (see section 4). You have to pay to send children to these schools.

RELIGIOUS SCHOOLS/FAITH SCHOOLS.

Maintained faith schools are like all other maintained schools in a number of ways. They must:

- follow the National Curriculum
- participate in National Curriculum tests and assessments
- be inspected by Ofsted regularly
- follow the School Admissions Code
- There are about 7,000 state faith schools in England (DFE statistics 2011)
- About 68% are Church of England and 30% Catholic
- There are also Jewish, Muslim and Sikh schools
- If one of these schools is being considered for your child, checks need to be made about the admission policy, especially if you live outside the area
- The Government is happy to see an expansion of these schools and they can become Academies
- State faith schools receive most of their funding from the Government
- Although faith schools may give priority to applicants who are of the faith of the school, they must admit other applicants if they cannot fill all of their places with children of that faith
- The final decision for admissions rests with the governors.

ADDITIONAL PROVISION

Pupil Referral Units (PRUs) and other alternative provision providers cater for vulnerable pupils who do not attend mainstream schools because of behaviour, exclusion, illness, teenage pregnancy, or because they do not have a school place. Figures published for the first time last year show that in 2010, only 1.4 per cent of pupils in alternative provision achieved five or more GCSEs at grade A*-C, or equivalent, including English and mathematics. This compares with 53.4 per cent in all schools in England. What often isn't taken into account however, is that many of the young people in PRUs are often school refusers, excluded pupils or disruptive and it tends to be forgotten that some 60% of PRUs were rated as Good or Outstanding by Ofsted. No mean achievement when you're dealing with challenging, disaffected young people who could not cope at their previous schools. Many Local Authorities have established Pupil Referral Units (PRUs) in their areas for the purposes of educating young people who have either been excluded from school or are at risk of exclusion (see section 18). These are sometimes attached to local schools but are also found in designated buildings quite separate from them. PRUs can provide full or part-time education.

The Government's Behaviour Advisor Charlie Taylor has called on the best Pupil Referral Units (PRUs) to take advantage of Academy freedoms, to drive up quality of education and develop closer relationships with schools in their area.

SPECIAL SCHOOLS

Special schools usually take children with particular types of special needs. Many maintained schools also have special provision for children with particular needs. For example, they may have good access for physically disabled pupils or special teaching for pupils with hearing, sight difficulties or dyslexia. You can ask to see a school's policy on SEN to make sure you know what can be offered. You can also arrange to visit a number of schools if you want to. In 2011 more than 600 Special Schools were registered with the Department for Education in England.

Some children, whose needs are so complex that it is extremely difficult to cater for them in mainstream education, will probably attend special schools. There are now far fewer special schools because many pupils who previously attended them are educated in mainstream schools. However there are still more than 90,000 children in special schools with 2,000 also attending mainstream schools for part of their timetable.

The major difference between all these schools is the way they are funded and supported not what or how they teach. If you would like further information on the range and type of schools offered go to **www.direct.gov.uk/en/parents or www.parentscentre.gov.uk** which give helpful advice on a range of subjects, including varieties of school and admission arrangements.

3. FURTHER EDUCATION.
END OF KEY STAGE 4 - SIXTH FORM SCHOOL OR COLLEGE

At the end of Year 11 pupils can officially leave school but it has now been decided that from 2015 it will be compulsory for young people to stay in education, training or employment until the age of eighteen. Continuing in Further Education, which may of course offer training opportunities, is already an extremely popular choice. This does not mean that all young people have to study A levels or re-sit GCSEs when they leave school but they must either be in some sort of work or training. It is proposed that anybody unwilling to take advantage of these options will find that their benefits are affected.

This measure is an attempt to reduce the number of aimless and often depressed young people in this category who are usually referred to as NEETs (Not in Education, Employment or Training) and guide them to a more positive future. Data from the DfE for 2011 shows that just under one million 16-24 year olds were recorded as NEETs in England alone. This remains a serious problem and as any parent or carer is well aware, young people with no hope too often turn to criminal activity as a consequence.

> The leaving date, for those students in year 11, is normally the last Friday in June even if the young person is sixteen before that date. They do not have to attend a sixth form school or college but most choose to stay in some form of education. Remember that Key Stage 4 passes extremely quickly, and planning for life after Year 11 needs to start at the beginning of Year 10. Some sixth form (Further Education) colleges are extremely popular and applications need to be in early to be sure of a place. If the young person in your care is staying on at the sixth form of the school they have been attending, information should be sent to you and there will be opportunities to talk to your child's teachers about what is on offer. Young people will want to be closely involved in discussions about what is a crucial point in their lives.

There have been major changes to sixth form and Further Education provision during the last few years. The range of courses is massive these days and new subjects will appear that may not have been taught in Key Stage 3 or 4, such as Psychology or Classical Civilisation as well as Dance, Communication Studies and subjects that will link to jobs and the workplace generally.

If a young person is considering staying in education beyond the age of 16, all concerned need to understand and accept what is involved.

- The young person should be persuaded to start gathering information as early as year 10, about the opportunities available
- Discuss the alternatives with any professional who has an understanding of 11-19 education
- Listen to the advice of other parents whose children have experienced further education or sixth form studies
- You must listen carefully to the views of the young person in your care but also make sure they fully understand the significance of the choices they make.

A and AS LEVELS.

"A" Levels still exist but they are split into two parts.

1. Advanced Subsidiary (AS) levels are usually taken in the first year of sixth form (Year 12) and are worth half an "A" level.

2. A2 exams are taken in the second year (Year 13). These are similar to what many of you will probably remember as the old "A" levels.

AS and A2 exams are considered to be the conventional academic route, not unlike the examination introduced in the 1950s. A significant difference, however, is that candidates can now take some units as they progress through the two years of 6th form rather than just sitting a single examination at the end of the course. Since Summer 2010 the grade of A* has been awarded at A level but this does not apply to AS levels.

Typically a student who has performed well at GCSE is likely to take between three and five AS levels in the first year of sixth form. After the results of those exams are published, in the following August, the student may decide in negotiation with teachers and those with parental responsibility that they only want to pursue three of the original five to A2. However a strong performance at AS examinations may see them continuing with all five. The International Baccalaureate is offered as an alternative to "A" levels in some schools or colleges. This is a two year diploma widely recognised by many leading universities **(see www.ibo.org/diploma).**

Apprenticeship programmes have been introduced and are designed for young people and adults from 16 -24 years of age. If you are looking to be employed in the workplace, with a wage or training allowance, but want to combine this with training and the achievement of recognised qualifications see **(http://www.apprenticeships.org.uk/Be-An-Apprentice/)**

However in September 2008 a new qualification for 14 to 19 year olds was made available. This is simply called The Diploma and is designed to combine work related skills in a practical, creative and enjoyable way. To help you research this course go to **http://yp.direct.gov.uk/diplomas/**

There may be confusion about these different approaches, as with the introduction of any new examination, but it does represent a serious attempt to redress the balance between academic and vocational courses. Vocational routes into higher education have until recently been regarded as the poor relation when compared to traditional academic approaches.

If the young person in your care is considering university they must be advised to research the courses on offer early. The application procedure is a complex process, which demands determination and perseverance. The university or college prospectus is essential reading which will not only describe the content of courses and entry requirements, but availability and range of accommodation, social activities, financial issues and the open days on which potential students can visit. Although colleges and schools are generally extremely supportive in the application process, researching a university place needs to take a high priority in the first year of sixth form (Year 12).

4. NATIONAL CURRICULUM.

The National Curriculum has to be followed by all state schools in England, Wales and Northern Ireland. It tells schools what children must study and what they should know at certain ages. Children are tested at various stages to keep a check on standards although the Welsh Assembly abandoned Standard Assessment Tests (SATs - see section 7) as long ago as 2007, replacing them with a different form of assessment.

- The core subjects, English, Maths and Science are compulsory from the age of 5 through to 16. Schools spend a lot of time teaching reading, writing and number during the week although this may be referred to as numeracy and literacy. Primary schools normally have literacy and numeracy sessions every day
- It has recently been announced that from 2014 Modern Foreign Languages will become compulsory for children in maintained schools from the age of seven
- The next group is called the foundation subjects, which must be taught in state schools. They are History, Geography, Music, Physical Education (PE), ICT, Art, Design Technology and in addition for secondary school pupils, Citizenship and Modern Foreign Languages
- Careers Education and Work Related Learning are now taught in secondary schools
- Religious education and sex education also form part of the curriculum. It is possible to withdraw children from these lessons, apart from the biological aspects of human growth and reproduction, taught as part of the national curriculum
- All maintained schools must provide daily collective worship for their pupils. This is currently under review.

5. TEACHING METHODS.

"That's not the way we did it!"

It is not unusual for parents to criticise the way subjects are taught "these days" but what has to be accepted is that there have been many changes since we were at school however much we may dislike them. Forcing your ideas on to a child who is being taught another way in class can be disastrous. You may not be convinced that the modern methods being used in the school are effective but you have to put yourself in the child or teacher's shoes and step back a little before you make judgements. It is uncomfortable and sometimes upsetting for children when their teacher is criticised. Even worse it may lead to a child developing negative attitudes towards the teacher and school. It can be difficult to give full and positive support to methods you don't really approve of but if your child is making progress and is happy, then your feelings are best left to one side. If you don't have confidence in what is happening at school, for example if the child in your care is rather slower with their reading progress than others, that would be a cause for concern. A quiet chat with the class or subject teacher might be enough to give greater urgency to the situation but it also has to be acknowledged that there are occasions when schools fail to respond properly to the genuine concerns of parents and carers.

> Schools are now giving much more information about what is taught and what teaching strategies they use. This can come in the form of taster sessions for adults and open evenings where you can see children at work; as well as information evenings, open days, handbooks and other documents about how the school is organised and run. The more you can become familiar with any of these, the more comfortable you are likely to feel with the systems.
>
> Some information can be explained very easily. For example literacy is just another term for reading and writing, and numeracy is maths, but it is sometimes much more difficult to understand how and why children are put into certain teaching groups.

TEACHING GROUPS

- Mixed ability groups - all children are taught together whatever their ability.

- Setting - the children will be split into teaching groups, for subjects, depending on their ability. This happens most often in English and Maths in the primary school but is used for a wider range of subjects in the secondary school.

- Banding - is probably the most difficult form of grouping to understand and is commonly found in secondary schools. Basically a year group of children, let's say 240, is split into broad bands of ability using information the school has, e.g. Sats scores, reading, writing, school test results and teachers' comments etc. This can then be used to create 3 bands, usually higher, middle and lower. Because it is generally felt that children in the lower bands need more support there are often fewer pupils in that band, so the split might be, 100 in the higher band, 80 in the middle and 60 in the lower band. These bands are then taught together for many of their subjects. Please remember this is only an example of the way some schools organise their teaching groups, they might for example have 2 or 4 bands. It is really up to individual schools to respond to your concerns and explain exactly what is happening. You must keep asking if you are confused.

6. WHAT IS A KEY STAGE?

- A Key Stage in school is linked to a child's age.
- There are four Key Stages after the Foundation Stage (see section 7)

- KS1 is from 5-7.   • KS2 is from 7-11.   • KS3 is from 11-14.   • KS4 is from 14-16.

STAGES, YEARS, NATIONAL TESTS AND TASKS

Age	Stage	Year	Tests	Tests
3-4 4-5	Foundation	Reception	Early Years Foundation Profile. Teacher report.	Levels 1-3 Average level 2
5-6 6-7	Key Stage 1	Year 1 Year 2	National tests and tasks in English and Maths. This does not apply in Wales.	
7-8 8-9 9-10 10-11	Key Stage 2	Year 3 Year 4 Year 5 Year 6	National tests in English, Maths and Science.	Levels 2-5 Average level 4
11-12 12-13 13-14	Key Stage 3	Year 7 Year 8 Year 9	No National Tests. Schools conduct own internal testing and exams.	
14-15 15-16	Key Stage 4	Year 10 Year 11	Most children take GCSEs or other nationally recognised vocational qualifications.	GCSE exams are externally marked and graded A*- G

On completion of key stage 4 they will take national examinations, usually GCSEs although there are proposals to change these exams by 2014 (see Section 7). Wales abandoned SATs in 2008 to be replaced by a different form of assessment. There has been fierce resistance to such a change in England.

This has further accentuated the difference between the English and Welsh systems although the General Teaching Council in England (GTC-disbanded in 2012), which was the teaching equivalent of the General Medical Council, had called for a complete overhaul of testing and league tables. Reviews of what should be taught through the National Curriculum are currently taking place and if the proposals are adopted will become compulsory from 2014.

7. EXAMS AND TESTING.

EARLY YEARS FOUNDATION STAGE

The foundation stage covers structured learning for children from birth to the end of reception year. Children's learning is planned and assessed through a number of areas. From September 2012 there will be seven areas of learning: Three prime areas – communication and language; physical development, and personal social and emotional development; and four specific areas – literacy; mathematics, understanding the world and expressive arts and design. All registered early years providers must use this framework but they do not apply to toddler groups, nannies or short term care.

> The Early Learning Goals are designed to help to lay solid foundations for future learning; especially for those children who have not benefited from high-quality early years experience, have special needs or speak English as an additional language. Very young children will be guided towards the learning goals by identifying and monitoring the knowledge, skills, understanding and attitude that children need if they are to achieve the early learning targets by the end of the Foundation Stage. It should be noted that the Welsh Assembly has combined the Foundation Stage with early years education and Key Stage 1 to support all children between the ages of three and seven.

Since 2003 teachers of children within this stage in England have been required to complete a foundation stage profile for each child. In September 2012 the profile changed and now assesses pupils against 17 goals instead of the 69 previously used. For each goal teachers will have to decide whether children are meeting the expected levels. A short written summary of progress must be provided to parents or carers when the child reaches the age of two. At the end of the foundation stage the information can be passed to Year 1 teachers to help the child continue with their progress.

KEY STAGE 1 - The assessment of reading, writing and number continues. This, together with evidence gathered during the foundation stage, is used to give teachers more information about your child as well as to set targets for future progression. At the end of this key stage in England there is a national test, called a Standard Assessment Test (SAT), in Maths and English. At this stage children are assessed by their teachers who observe them undertaking classroom based tasks and make a judgement about the level they have reached. The results are given in levels and most children are expected to have reached level 2 by the age of 7. Children in Wales are not tested at the end of Key Stage 1 but information gathered from this stage and early years' education is used to establish what progress your child is making.

KEY STAGE 2 - Teaching style and assessment becomes more formal during this stage and In England these children take a SAT in Year 6 of primary school. These tests at Key Stage 2 currently apply to all English schools within the state system. As well as being tested in Maths and English, a teacher assessment in Science is also included. Most children are expected to have achieved level 4 by the end of Key Stage 2. Children take a written examination in Maths and English and the papers are marked by examiners not connected with the school.

KEY STAGE 3 - Having completed Key Stage 2 most children transfer to secondary education but there are exceptions in some parts of the country where there is a three-part system in operation, of primary, middle and upper schools. Years 7, 8 and 9 form Key Stage 3. There are no formal examinations at the end of this key stage but there will be school assessments in years 7, 8 and 9 along with reports on progress and the levels achieved.

KEY STAGE 4 - This is the stage during which students study GCSE, as well as other examination and vocational courses, chosen in year 9. In addition to the traditional GCSEs, vocational courses can also be offered, closely linked to the world of work. For those who feel they cannot cope with these courses, foundation apprenticeships are being developed. Many young people now have the opportunity to attend college during the school week and most others will take part in work experience during the 10th or 11th year. The results of GCSE examinations are given in grades A*-G not levels.

Please note that major changes are proposed for GCSEs and if the recommendations are accepted students may start studying for the new style exam from 2014 and take the new exam in 2016.

8. EXAM REVISION.

One of the most stressful times of the year for families is exam time, but research has shown that when carers and parents get involved with their children's exam preparation, results are likely to improve. There are things that you can do to help young people achieve better results. First you need to know how the young person in your care reacts to exams. However they cope, the whole family will probably heave a sigh of relief when the exams are over. But in the meantime, what can you do to help?

- Recognise how important these exams are and how much time will be needed if they are to do well - don't make too many demands during this period and the 'tidy bed room' argument might best be put on hold for a while
- Encourage the rest of the family to help by not disturbing revision - provide a quiet place for study, where work can be safely kept
- Encourage relaxation time. Young people need regular breaks during revision to go for a walk or listen to some music. This will help them start the next revision period refreshed
- Try not to discourage them from socialising with their friends although group revision in the local park for the maths exam may not be such a good idea!
- Make sure you motivate and be positive – praise and rewards work well
- Emphasise the need for plenty of sleep – the tendency amongst many young people is to stay awake all night in the hope of catching up on any learning they may have missed – this is not a good idea. They must get enough sleep or they may arrive at the exam feeling tired and anxious
- Make sure that they are eating a healthy, balanced diet. It is quite common for exam stress to lead to a loss of appetite; tempt them with foods they like
- Help them to forget about each exam as it is finished – have a calendar with the exam dates marked on and get a thick black marker to cross off exam days once they are over
- Don't keep questioning them about how well they think they've done. It won't change the result!
- Make sure that you know exactly when the exams are. A significant number of students turn up at the wrong time. They will not be allowed to take the exam!

As a carer you can also give young people some tips to help with revision:

- Plan for 30-45 minute revision sessions, any longer and it is likely that nothing more will sink in; advise a short break between sessions
- In the evenings after school, plan to revise one or two subjects only, leaving some time for relaxation
- Organise the paperwork subject by subject and keep it separate
- Throw out or store the paperwork not needed but make sure it really isn't needed! Any work stored on a computer must be backed up
- Plan to revise specific topics in each subject, not everything at once
- Ensure that each session starts by tackling the most difficult bits
- Plan to cover each subject several times and revisit each one nearer the exams
- Revising with loud music or television on is not a good idea, but having some music in the background may help
- Just reading through revision material is generally not enough. Making brief notes in either words or pictures is a much better aid to memory
- Have all the books needed to hand
- Working with a friend can be useful because it allows them to test each other, talk about the work and discover that everyone is as stressed as they are
- Post-it labels around the house with useful facts on can also be helpful.

> Remember, exams are not necessarily a true indication of how intelligent your child is. It is not the end of the world if they don't get the results they or you want and expect, and there are always other options open to them. Most public exams can be taken at any age; it just makes life that much easier for everybody, if they are satisfactorily completed at the earliest opportunity.

9. TRANSITION.

Transition is change from one educational stage to another. In schools it is mentioned most commonly when young people are moving from primary to secondary school but there are other important points in schools when major changes occur. Children will cope better if they are well prepared for them. We are going to focus on four major transitions that most children have to encounter, although it's important to remember that it might be slightly different in some parts of the country, where for example there are middle schools (see section 2). Nearly all schools these days take great care to give parents/carers excellent information about these transitions, either through letters home, meetings or both.

INFANT TO JUNIOR.

After three years in the infant school, at the end of Key Stage 1 (see section 6) children will move from the infant department to the junior department of their primary school. Often they will stay in the same building but sometimes there are separate infant and junior sites. So what changes might you notice when children start Key Stage 2?

- There may be no afternoon playtime
- Children are likely to spend more time in formal situations such as silent reading and independent working
- Teachers will be encouraging them to think more for themselves
- Sometimes the school day is slightly longer
- There may be changes in the amount and type of homework
- They will be encouraged to take responsibility for day-to-day organisation such as remembering games kit and taking letters home

Don't panic! Most of these changes will be gradual, but remember, lots of advice and support will be necessary, especially from you. Searching school bags for important information will become a way of life!

PRIMARY TO SECONDARY.

In the final year of primary school, in Year 6, most children will prepare to move on to secondary school. This is the end of Key Stage 2 and pupils in England will be assessed in English, Maths and Science (see section 7) in the summer term. Schools have lots of experience at preparing children to move on and you will be given help and information in order to make sure all goes as smoothly as possible.

> Teachers know that children are often very anxious as well as being excited about moving to "big school." They will have heard all sorts of rumours about what's going to happen to them when they arrive. Having your head pushed down the toilet and being thrown into ponds or prickly bushes seem to feature, as well as the bullying tales and the monsters they're going to have for teachers. It's not surprising that these children have a few concerns about transferring. A lot of effort is made to remove any fear before this change and to prepare them for the differences between primary and secondary. Many schools start this preparation in Year 5 of primary school, or even earlier, because they want to make the children feel really comfortable with what is going to happen as they move into Key Stage 3.

To make this process easier for parents/carers and pupils most schools use a variety of strategies including:

- Regular visits, with their class teacher, to the secondary school
- Visits from the secondary teachers to the primary school
- Taster days where the children can sample the sort of lessons they will be taught at the secondary school
- Invitations to drama, music and sports events at the secondary school
- Open days for parents/carers and pupils. Sometimes this happens during a normal working day so that you can see pupils in their lessons
- Open evenings, which will give you a chance to talk to teachers and other pupils
- Handbooks and guides that will help you understand how the new school works
- Primary school records which are passed to the secondary school.

It has to be remembered that for Looked after Children transition can be even more complicated because of other changes they may be experiencing at the same time. Careful planning for transfer from primary to secondary school counts for very little if the young person is moved out of area at the end of Year 6, and is expected to settle into a completely unfamiliar secondary environment a few weeks later. What may appear to be a simple task such as passing primary school records on to the new secondary school can suddenly become a difficult and lengthy operation.

On arriving at secondary school the young people will find themselves part of a number of different groups, e.g. form or tutor groups, ability groups and subject groups. The other main changes that children will have to be ready for when they arrive at secondary school are likely to be some of the following:

- It will usually be a much bigger school
- They will have a timetable to follow so organisation will be really important
- If there are lockers in the school the children can store books and equipment in them. If not they will have to carry quite a lot around during the day. Again organisation is vital to avoid mislaid equipment and a bad back!
- They may work with up to 10 or even 12 different teachers during the week
- They are likely to be in a form group with a teacher but they may not be taught in that group. It is quite possible that their form teacher will not actually teach them and will rely on talking to teaching colleagues and support teachers to build a better picture of each child
- They might be taught new subjects such as languages and different types of technology
- They might find themselves in different teaching groups for certain subjects because the school uses setting, banding or mixed ability (See section 5)
- Travelling to the new school could be more complicated needing planning and support from you
- It isn't always possible for children to be in forms or teaching groups with their friends from primary school. However most children do make new friendships very quickly
- There will be more homework. A great many schools now run after school homework clubs and other sessions to support children.

During the early years of secondary school you will often find that many children tell you very little about school, especially if there are problems. This is all part of adolescence and can be very painful for everybody involved. It's important that they take more responsibility for organising themselves, packing school bags, getting themselves to school on time, making sure you receive important letters from the school about trips, exams, holidays etc. This is all about growing up and creating space to live in a world in which they don't want you to interfere too much.

> Young people are not likely to admit it but they still want and need your support. Keeping your eye on what's going on, without making it too obvious, is a skill that carers have developed over generations. Looking for non-verbal clues to serious problems like bullying is especially important. The smiley, talkative, open child who suddenly becomes sullen, withdrawn and secretive may not just be experiencing adolescence.

Checking that they have packed that P.E. kit or homework and that there are no important letters lurking at the bottom of the school bag can save a lot of trouble later. There are times when you have to interfere but knowing when to back off, particularly during the teenage years, is just as important.

OPTIONS - YEAR 9 - KEY STAGE 3 to KEY STAGE 4.

They are now ready to move onto Key Stage 4 courses in Years 10 and 11. During the first half of Year 9 students have to choose which subjects they want to take, which will depend very much on their strengths. There will usually be a Key Stage 4 evening, sometimes called Options evening, when the process will be explained. Most schools send a booklet home to give more detailed information about subject choices and what they lead to.

> It's really important to attend these meetings, read the information and take advice, bearing in mind what the child wants to do at the end of Year 11, when education is no longer compulsory. Good schools give their students lots of help and involve them in any decisions. During Key Stage 4 you can expect to see an increase in homework as well as coursework, which counts towards the final exam mark. Many young people cope pretty well with exam stress but others need lots of TLC. Getting the balance right between interfering and keeping a watchful eye is important but never easy. Knowing the strengths, needs, ambitions and hopes of the young person in your care is always vital and an essential contribution at this stage but what you see as help can look like interference to a growling adolescent!
>
> Helpful information can also be found at the DFE website on
> **www.direct.gov.uk/en/parents/**

It will worry you just as much if the child you are caring for doesn't seem to be doing any work at all. The, "Haven't you got any homework?" or "I never see you doing any homework!" discussion is well known in lots of families. The answers, "We never get any," "I did it in the library," "Finished it in class," as well as lots of unprintable ones, are just as well known. The screaming rows that often follow usually don't get anywhere. If a young person of this age wants to hide something from you they probably can. Good communications with the school (see sections 14 and 15) and an understanding of what should be happening in school, as well as how the young person is coping might not stop the rows but it will give some ideas about what to do next. The LAC review during this period becomes vitally important to ensure that proper consideration is given to educational plans for Key Stage 4, which can then be supported by the Personal Education Plan (PEP) and the Care Plan.

END OF KEY STAGE 4 to SIXTH FORM SCHOOL OR COLLEGE.

Young people will want to be closely involved in this transition because it is such a crucial point in their lives, but close reference should also be made to Pathways Planning and the Care Plan as well as any arrangements that might be in place for leaving care. Difficulties could arise because the young person is moving out of the area after Year 11, in which case planning and organisation take on an even greater significance.

> Making the best choices for the young person in your care, as they move into Further Education is not easy. Go to the open evenings, talk to parents and students who have had experience of the different subjects and systems, but don't leave it too late because options might start disappearing as college places begin to fill up. It must be remembered that final decisions can only be made with the consent and agreement of birth parents.

10. HOME-SCHOOL AGREEMENTS.

In the last few years schools have made great efforts to communicate more effectively with parents and carers. There is now a recognition that if young people are to perform well in school then the development of a solid partnership between parents/guardians, pupils, teachers and all those who are called upon to support the child in your care, is extremely important. Parents and carers often establish strong links with primary schools for a variety of reasons, not least of which is a desire from the children themselves for parents to become involved. Older children, usually at secondary schools, are much less likely to encourage too much involvement with school and in many cases give very little information about what is happening on a daily basis.

Home-school agreements have gone some way to filling the information gap experienced by parents/carers who were unable or perhaps unwilling to have too much contact with their child's school. Schools are now called upon to adopt a home-school agreement along with a parental declaration of support. The agreement should explain:

- The ethos of the school
- The importance of, and responsibility for, regular and punctual attendance
- The importance of, and responsibility for, good discipline and behaviour
- What is expected from schools, parents and pupils in relation to homework
- The information schools and parents will give one another.

> Once this is agreed and adopted by the governing body (see Section 11), reasonable steps are then taken to ensure that all registered parents of pupils of school age sign a declaration to indicate that they understand and accept the agreement. It is made absolutely clear that no child or parent should suffer any consequences if there is a failure or refusal to sign the agreement. Neither can the agreement be used as a condition of a child being admitted to a school, although a parent or guardian may routinely be asked to sign such a document during the admission process.

It is probably unnecessary to expand on all the areas above in too much detail but it may be worth making further reference to attendance, discipline and behaviour, and homework. The first two have been particularly highlighted by the Government and extensively covered by the media as part of a drive to reduce truancy and anti-social behaviour. Homework has been the cause of a fair degree of conflict over the years between home and school, so a brief look at DFE recommendations may help to bring some clarity to the issue. Much more detailed information about these agreements is available on the DFE site: **www.direct.gov.uk/homeschoolagreement**

REGULAR AND PUNCTUAL ATTENDANCE.

Figures released by the Department for Education in 2011 show that around 66,000 pupils of all ages skipped school sessions without permission on a typical day in 2009-10 through truancy, family holidays, illness and other reasons. The analysis also alarmingly revealed that truancy amongst primary age children reached record levels in that year.

It goes without saying that poor attendance has an impact on performance at school. Quite apart from the subject content missed because of absence, non-attendance at school can have a dramatic effect on relationships both with friends and teachers. Lateness and absence can grow to be habits, which are difficult to break unless there is a major effort not only from the pupil but also from teachers and parents. Poor punctuality may seem less disturbing than non-attendance but there are young people, mainly but not always, in secondary schools, who arrive so late at school that they have effectively missed the morning's lessons. Of course there will be a variety of reasons why this is happening and this should form part of a thorough investigation, but the central issue remains that you are responsible for ensuring that the child in your care receives full-time education. Not surprisingly there is a very strong link between poor attendance and under achievement in schools.

> Parents and carers are also responsible for informing school when their child is unable to attend. This does not relieve schools of their responsibility to alert parents when they detect a pattern of absence or poor punctuality. Indeed schools throughout the country in partnership with home, the police, social services and Education Welfare Officers (EWOs - see section 14) are working hard to improve levels of attendance and punctuality. The government has also recently made it clear that there is no absolute right to take children on holiday during term time and ministers are trying to discourage families from doing so. Permission must be granted by the school; if that is not the case then the absence is likely be recorded as unauthorised.

There are many reasons why parents will want to take their children out of school during term time but proper dialogue with the school is the best way forward. Confusion can usually be avoided by informing the school of your plans and filling in the appropriate forms requesting a period of absence for your child. If the period requested exceeds ten days then the head teacher may not give approval.

HOMEWORK.

Homework is often a source of friction, more often between older pupils and their parents or teachers. Within home-school agreements the government suggests that schools spell out the homework policy so that you are able to establish approximately what your child should be doing at home on a weekly basis. Of course a really evasive student can always find a good excuse for doing very little homework.

> It is impossible to check everything your child is supposed to be doing at school and most parents/ carers would find it very difficult to discover the truth in many cases. Close contact with school can usually establish what is happening but it is unwise to wait until parents' evening (see Section 17) before raising any concerns. There is likely to be some sort of planner or diary recording homework, which you may be asked to sign, but they are only as reliable as the child. They are frequently mislaid and don't always contain accurate information about what work should be completed. Some schools now put homework on-line and use e-mail and text communications to deal with problems and queries.

HOMEWORK GUIDANCE

PRIMARY	
Years 1 and 2	1 hour a week (Reading, spelling, other literacy work and number work)
Years 3 and 4	1.5 hours a week (literacy and numeracy work, occasional assignments in other subjects
Years 5 and 6	30 minutes a day (Regular weekly schedule with continued emphasis on literacy and numeracy but also ranging widely over the curriculum)
SECONDARY	
Years 7 and 8	45 - 90 minutes a day.
Year 9	1 hour a day
Year 10 and 11	1.5 - 2.5 hours a day.

Please remember that this is only guidance, proposed by the previous government, and schools are free to develop homework policies in a way that is most appropriate to the needs of their students. Some researchers suggest that homework should be abandoned altogether whilst a study of 3000 children conducted for the DFE in 2012 concluded that two hours homework a night is strongly linked to much better achievement in English, Maths and Science. The key would seem to be consultation at all levels within the school community. Best practice suggests this should include pupils, followed by the effective communication of proposals and agreed policies so that everybody understands their role in the process. For further information see: **www.parentscentre.gov.uk/educationandlearning**

DISCIPLINE AND BEHAVIOUR.

It is inevitable that home-school agreements will focus on discipline and it is the responsibility of the school to have in place a behaviour policy that is supported by governors and parents. It should be clearly communicated to all involved what expectations the school will have of its pupils, and how those with parental responsibility can demonstrate their support for upholding those standards. Detention is commonly used in schools and head teachers do have the right to detain your child at the end of the school day. They no longer have to give 24 hours notice of detention although most schools would prefer to do so for safety reasons. However, they must ensure that:

- All parents/carers have been made aware that this sanction might be used
- The detention is given by a member of staff authorised by the head to do so
- The age of the pupil is taken into account
- Any medical, travel, religious or special needs are given proper consideration
- The detention is reasonable and proportionate to the offence.

You can object to detention being used and provide information supporting your case to the head teacher for consideration but it is always worth reflecting firstly on whether the punishment is fair, and secondly whether it might be effective in changing the behaviour of the young person. Most teachers use detentions because they want to see an improvement in a pupil's attitude or behaviour. You would be more concerned if a teacher was to do nothing about persistent lateness, poor behaviour or failure to produce homework. If you do feel that punishments are excessive talk to class teachers/form tutors/heads of year or senior staff to get a full picture of what is happening. It is unwise to react without knowing all the facts.

The coalition government has restated the fact that all schools must have measures in place to encourage good behaviour and prevent all forms of bullying. An anti-bullying policy should form part of the code of conduct, and that of course encompasses a whole range of behavioural issues that the school should clarify within its policy including racism, violence or threatening behaviour, the use of drugs or alcohol and sexual harassment. Many schools also give excellent advice about online bullying (see section 21) which covers both use of the internet and mobile phones. For further information it is worth reading the DFE booklet produced in 2011 entitled **"Preventing and Tackling Bullying."**

Most schools are looking for self-discipline from their students rather than imposed discipline but it is inevitable that there will be occasions when the school has to intervene because students engage in unacceptable behaviour. Exclusion may form a part of the policy (see section 18) but this is only one way of tackling poor behaviour. All parents should look carefully at school documentation in order to identify what disciplinary measures are used within the school. Schools use a whole range of sanctions to tackle indiscipline but there are no regulations that determine exactly what form these should take, other than to require the school to stay within the law when deciding what is reasonable as a punishment.

It should also be noted that since 2006 head teachers have had the power by law to "regulate" pupils' conduct when they are not on school premises. This could mean a school investigation into trouble at the local shops or when pupils are travelling to and from school. Head teachers can refer the matter to the police should they believe the behaviour to be criminal. The DFE guidance of 2012 also makes it clear that teachers have legal powers to use reasonable force when removing a child from a classroom or preventing a child from leaving. It has to be said most teachers would avoid physical contact if at all possible although previously many have tried to intervene in fights or arguments not knowing whether the law would protect them should there be an injury. Bags can also be searched to ensure that dangerous, illegal or banned items are not brought onto school premises.

There have been a number of high profile cases involving teachers punishing pupils, and what has become clear is that prosecutions will be pursued against teachers or other members of staff whose actions are felt to be unreasonable. Should there be an incident involving your child it is vitally important that you establish exactly what happened before reacting. A calm, informed approach to the school, outlining your grievance and asking for an investigation, is usually productive. If that fails then you may have to use other courses of action such as the governing body, or in extreme cases local politicians, but always try and give the school an opportunity to respond to your complaints (see Section 22) in the first instance. Over- aggression in these cases can lead to permanently damaged relationships between home and school, which serves nobody's interests.

Although the DFE in its **"School Uniform Guidance-2012"** strongly encourages schools to have a uniform there is no legislation that deals exclusively with the issue. Many schools believe that school uniform is helpful in promoting effective teaching and learning although that's not a view supported by all schools. Governing bodies decide whether or not there will be a uniform and just as the maintenance of discipline is part of the head teacher's responsibility, so is the insistence that it is worn appropriately. Pupils can be disciplined for breaches of uniform policy and sometimes sent home to correct a breach of that policy, but the DFE does not consider exclusion to be appropriate unless it forms part of a pattern of "defiant behaviour" generally.

11. GOVERNING BODIES OF SCHOOLS.

The governing body is ultimately responsible for a school's performance. The composition of the governing body will vary depending on the school but there are places for parents or those with parental responsibility, staff, Local Authority, maintained schools and representatives of the community. The DFE outlines the duties that the governing body must, in law, undertake and those it must delegate to the head teacher. Ideally, governing bodies and head teachers should work together in partnership to develop key policies such as discipline and attendance strategies but the head teacher and the professional staff are accountable to the governing body. The school's Development Plan, Improvement Plan or post-Ofsted Action Plan after an inspection by Ofsted are usually developed through close consultation between head teachers and their governing bodies.

Governors:
- Set suitable aims and objectives
- Agree policies, targets and priorities
- Monitor and review aims and objectives as well as determining whether policies, targets and priorities are being achieved or implemented

The head teacher:
- Carries out many responsibilities on behalf of the governing body
- Is the lead professional who will be responsible for ensuring that policies are implemented and targets achieved.

Further information about governing bodies can be obtained from **www.direct.gov.uk** (Education and Learning)

12. SPECIAL EDUCATIONAL NEEDS (SEN).

Many people think that this term only applies to those children who have serious difficulties in school. In fact it covers all children who it is believed need extra support and help with their studies, because they are struggling to progress at a similar rate to the majority of their peers. Most of these children are in mainstream schools (see section 2) and their needs may have been noticed, often by carers and parents, because they have physical, learning, emotional or behavioural difficulties that have prevented them making reasonable progress. It is estimated that about 20% of children will need extra help at some point in their school lives. So many children have access to special needs support that there should be no stigma or embarrassment attached to the process. Some will have a wide range of problems whilst other children just need help in very specific areas for a limited time. An important element of the Special Educational Needs Co-ordinator's (SENCO -see section 14) role is to maintain and update the special needs register. An excellent guide can be downloaded from the DFE entitled **"Special Educational Needs (SEN)-A Guide for Parents and Carers"** although it should be emphasised that this was published in 2009 and it is likely further changes will be introduced by 2014 along the lines of the proposals outlined below.

The Government believes that under the present system parents have a real struggle to get the help their children need so it is suggested that:

- Parent should be involved in the assessment process and be given control of the funding needed to support their child
- It should form part of a combined education, health and care plan
- School Action and Action plus (see below) should be replaced with one school based plan
- Teacher training on special needs should be improved
- Voluntary groups should be included
- Parents should be given a greater choice of school
- Parents and community groups should be given the power to set up special free schools (see section 2).

Until these changes take effect you will continue to hear teachers talk about the Code of Practice. The revised code was introduced for all schools from January 2002 and helps to identify, assess and follow the progress of these pupils. There is nothing to stop you raising your concerns if you feel the school hasn't noticed problems but try and do this by talking it through with the teachers involved rather than challenging their judgement or teaching. (See sections 14 and 15) The Code of Practice is designed to allow a young person to move between the levels set out below depending on the child's current needs and progress. The levels, which may well change following recent Government proposals, presently are:

SCHOOL ACTION - SCHOOL ACTION PLUS - STATEMENTED PROVISION

SCHOOL ACTION.

You or your child's teachers might be worried because:

- Very little progress is being made even though weaknesses have been recognised and worked on
- There are difficulties with reading, writing and/or maths
- Emotional or behavioural problems appear to be getting in the way of learning
- Even though specialist equipment is being used, physical problems are still preventing reasonable progress.

> School staff will discuss the problems with parents/carers and decide what type of support should be given. The staff most likely to be involved are the class or form teacher and other support teachers or assistants who know the child well and can make important contributions to the discussion. The Special Educational Needs Co-ordinator plays an important role managing and overseeing the process.

Having registered the child on the Code of Practice an Individual Education Plan (IEP) will usually be produced that sets out what support is needed. It might suggest:

- Different learning materials
- Special equipment
- Working in groups
- Individual support
- Support training for staff
- Support from the local authority
- Additional support from you either at home or in school.

The IEP is then reviewed every half term or term. A decision will be made whether to continue on this level, bring the child off altogether or move them on to the next level.

SCHOOL ACTION PLUS.

After this review it may be that there are still a number of worries and the teachers decide that more help is needed. They may ask for advice from an outside specialist such as a teacher from the local authority support services or an educational psychologist. Parents/carers will be involved in the discussions. In order to determine how to make progress, SENCO, teachers and specialists will put together a plan for the child, which could include:

- Looking at different ways of teaching the child
- Giving extra support (one to one or small group)
- Using other materials and equipment
- Getting a specialist to make an assessment
- Using lap-tops, spell- checkers and other technology.

Again there will be regular reviews and for many children the support given at Action Plus will help them improve enough to allow them to be taken out of the process. Some will remain on this level and a small number will need to move on to the next level, statementing.

STATEMENTED PROVISION.

If there has not been sufficient progress as a result of intervention during the first two stages, then a meeting should be arranged with all involved to decide whether it is necessary for the Local Authority to carry out a detailed assessment of the child's educational needs. Parents/Carers have the right to request this assessment but that does not always mean it will happen. Parental permission is needed for this process to take place.

The Authority will then collect together all the information and decide if a Statement of Special Educational Needs should be written. The information can be gathered from all those who have an interest in or knowledge of the young person.eg.

- School
- Birth parent
- Local Authority social worker
- Educational psychologist
- Speech therapist
- Health professional

Very often it is assumed that a carer's views are voiced by the social worker or the school. This is not always the case and it is vital that carers ensure that their opinions are sought and included.

> Statements set out the child's needs and all the special help they should be given but if the decision is not to issue a statement the authority must give reasons. The person with parental responsibility has the right to appeal to the Special Educational Needs Tribunal if they feel they have been unfairly treated, but it's worth knowing that only about 3% of children in England and Wales are statemented and the majority of special needs children are successfully catered for in schools, without a statement.

Statementing is often a lengthy process and can take up to six months even when all goes smoothly. It cannot take place without the consent of those with parental responsibility and birth parents must be kept informed of all developments. Once in place it is important to emphasise that a statement is a legal document, which describes how a young person's needs are to be met over a twelve-month period. After this period it must be reviewed. (See **www.direct.gov.uk/en/Parents** for further information)

13. WHAT IS INCLUSION?

Put simply it is the right to be educated in a mainstream school along with most other children. There are still a number of special schools for children who, because of their very specific needs, cannot attend a mainstream school, but inclusion means, "disabled and non-disabled young people learning together–enabling pupils to participate in the life and work of mainstream institutions to the best of their abilities, whatever their needs." (Centre for Studies on Inclusive Education). Schools are changing and learning to cope with the diverse needs presented by a wide range of children. The aim is also to give support and help to those young people who are more likely to drift away from education because their needs are not adequately addressed through mainstream provision.

> In January 2002 a new statutory framework came into force, which strengthened the rights of children with a statement of special educational needs (see section 12) to attend a mainstream school. Schools are, at the very least, requested to review their policies and decide what changes might need to be made in order to improve accessibility and inclusion; taking into account cost, practicability, health and safety, sustaining academic standards and the impact on other students.
>
> Part 1 of the Special Educational Needs and Disability Act 2001 states that all children with statements must be educated in a mainstream school unless this would be:
>
> Detrimental to the efficient education of other children,
> or:
> Against parental wishes.

The Equality Act of 2010 has further strengthened the discrimination laws making it unlawful for a school or any other education provider to treat a disabled student unfavourably. In the future, education providers will be obliged to provide extra support in the form of specialist teachers or equipment, although no date has yet been given for that proposal to be implemented.

The Local Authorities and schools outside their control can only refuse a place to a child with specific needs if it can demonstrate that there are no reasonable steps it could have taken which would avoid the placement adversely affecting the education of other children.

Schools are now much more accessible to students with special needs. This is partially due to changing attitudes but is also as a result of the pressure that has been applied to admit pupils who may formerly have been placed in special schools. Consequently many of these schools have closed in the last few years and those remaining mainly cater for children and young people whose needs are so complex that they cannot be accommodated in mainstream education.

> Emotional and behavioural problems are managed much more successfully in the mainstream than previously was the case, and there have been massive strides in the way schools, teachers and support workers have adapted to meet the needs of disabled children. There is also a body of evidence suggesting that inclusion is a value-added experience for the whole school community and encourages greater understanding of the difficulties that some children cope with on a daily basis.
>
> However there are criticisms of the inclusion policy, most of which relate to under resourcing and the extra pressures classroom teachers are exposed to through further training, preparation and planning.

14. WHO DO I NEED TO KNOW?

Schools are complicated organisations and the biggest problem is that although they are all similar in some ways no two schools are exactly alike. The one feature that remains the same is that all state schools and most others have a head teacher and some form of governing body. Apart from that, the way schools are organised can vary. Some large secondaries have a head teacher and three deputies, whilst in a small village primary school there might only be a head and perhaps one other teacher.

> The most important thing is for you to know which members of the school staff are going to be of greatest importance to you and the child in your care. In this section there is a brief description of a number of roles in school and the responsibilities attached to them. Some of these are common to both primary and secondary schools.
>
> You will probably prefer to contact the person you feel most comfortable with when approaching a school, but at least find out who the following are, and what connection they have with the child in your care. Many of them have daily contact with the children and will be very important figures in their lives.

THE DESIGNATED TEACHER

The designated teacher for Looked After Children may be a person with whom you come to have close links. Since 2009 all maintained schools have been required under the Children and Young Persons Act to have in place a designated teacher whose responsibility it is to promote the educational achievement of Looked After Children. It could be a head or deputy but is quite often a SENCO, (Special Educational Needs Co-ordinator) a Year Head, Head of a Key Stage or an experienced teacher who has specialist knowledge of the role. Their job is to make sure that Looked After Children get a reasonable deal out of school life. They will see that paper work is up to date, including Personal Education Plans (PEPs) and should have regular contact with social workers and other agencies involved in the Looked After Child's life.

THE CLASS TEACHER

The class teacher in a primary school is usually the first person you contact when you want information about your child's performance. That teacher is not only with the children as they arrive in the morning but teaches them most of their lessons as well. In addition to being responsible for your child's learning they will also take registers, deal with absence notes, sort out problems and generally try to make sure that the pupils in the class are cared for. Because they have so much contact with the children, class teachers often get to know them and their parents or carers really well.

THE FORM OR PASTORAL TUTOR

In secondary schools the form tutor is often the first teacher to turn to when you want information or have some concerns. They will see your child every day in registration. Form tutors have similar duties to the class teacher in a primary school but might not teach the children in their form. Because of this they will probably need to collect information about your child from other teachers and support staff. Sometimes these tutors stay with their groups throughout the secondary school and develop excellent relationships with the children in their forms.

CLASSROOM SUPPORT

This can come in a variety of forms but because these staff regularly work with individuals or small groups they usually develop very close relationships with the children. Class teachers and form tutors often ask for their help when they need more information about how the children get on with other children or adults. The information that support staff provide about progress or behaviour is crucial when completing reports or plans. There is a range of support in schools such as classroom assistants, learning mentors, support teachers and specialist teachers some of whom visit the school occasionally to help with the child's behavioural, emotional or health problems, as well as lack of progress.

THE YEAR HEAD OR HEAD OF KEY STAGE

You're more likely to find these roles in secondary schools but some primaries have a Head of Key Stage 1 or 2. You'll probably have some contact with these members of staff because they are the vital link into a year group and are heavily involved in admissions or inclusion. They can be dealing with between 100-300 children and can't be expected to have instant information about every child. However, like other senior members of the school staff, they are bound to get involved in serious incidents of bullying, violence or drug taking etc. Thankfully lots of Heads of Year also have opportunities to praise, reward and congratulate; a job they much prefer. Many, but not all, Heads of Year teach, but their main responsibility is to monitor the social and academic progress of the students in their care.

THE EDUCATIONAL WELFARE OFFICER (EWO)

EWOs are mainly involved with monitoring attendance and punctuality and are usually shared between schools. Where there are problems they will often call at a pupil's home to try and establish exactly what is happening. They aim to ensure that children attend school regularly and on time but if they discover that the problem is being caused by something that is happening in school e.g. bullying or problems with work, they liaise closely with teachers to establish what action can be taken. Many schools now have, or at least share, counsellors who do not teach but are trained to listen to children about their worries and problems.

THE SPECIAL EDUCATIONAL NEEDS CO-ORDINATOR

(SENCO) - There is a SENCO in all state schools and their job is to make sure that children with special educational needs receive the right level of help and support. If the young person in your care has identified special needs you will probably become very familiar with the SENCO but if they are making satisfactory progress there will be little or no contact. However some schools do assume that most Looked After Children have special needs, when it may be more appropriate for you to be discussing their progress with the Gifted and Talented co-ordinator, in order to ensure that some special skill or quality is nurtured and developed.

It would be wrong to suggest that these are the only members of a school staff you need to know, you might for example have a very good relationship with the head or subject teachers, but parents still arrive at parents' evenings not knowing the names of class teachers, form tutors and subject teachers, let alone the names of support staff. These members of staff are vitally important in a child's school life and knowing who they are shows that we as parents or carers recognise that importance. Getting to know staff on a more relaxed level through social events, sports teams, joining the Parent Teacher Association (PTA) and generally helping around the school is a brilliant way of supporting not only the school but also your child.

15. COMMUNICATIONS.

This is more about who to contact than who you know in a school. Basic accurate information about a child is essential but too often the details held by a school are incorrect or inadequate. The school office tends to be the place where most basic records are located, such as addresses and telephone numbers as well as emergency contacts. The staff in these offices will, in most cases, be the first people you speak to when you phone the school, and they will pass messages and information to teachers and other members of staff. It is important to make immediate contact with the school when you know the child in your care is going to be absent, because schools can be very quick to follow up the reasons for absence, especially if there is a history of truancy.

> You should make every effort to ensure that your children go to school every day. Not surprisingly there is a direct link between poor attendance and poor performance. But there are occasions when it's not possible for children to attend. If that's the case let the school know and do your best to ensure that missed work is completed. There will be times when you need to speak to a particular member of staff (see section 14) in order to give them confidential or sensitive information. Unless you have a direct line, phone the school office and explain that you need to speak to that member of staff urgently. The member of staff may not be able to speak to you straight away but should call back at the earliest opportunity.

Inform the school when:

- You change address or telephone number
- The emergency contact changes
- You know your child is going to be absent
- The absence is going to be for more than one day
- Someone else is going to pick the child up from school (This is mainly for younger children but can be important to an older child who is not supposed to have contact with some adults)
- They have to leave school early
- There is a medical problem, especially if attention is needed during the day. School staff will not give medicines or tablets to children.
- There is a problem at home, which might affect behaviour or progress in school: for example a contact visit
- There is a problem in school, which is causing unhappiness, especially if it involves bullying or racism.

It is a good idea to write to the school giving information, when you know in advance about absence or want to report a problem. Sometimes, however, serious situations just happen. School staff will be sympathetic in those circumstances but try and get messages to them so that they have some idea of what is going on.

Of course communications should not only be one way. Schools have a duty to keep you well informed through letters, reports, open evenings, calendars and review days etc, but they must also be able to make prompt contact with home where there's a pattern of unexplained absences, poor behaviour or lack of work. You can't police the children all the time and you should be able to expect a quick phone call, email or text to tell you when there are problems. Immediate contact between home and school at the first hint of trouble can save time and much bigger problems later. If you are concerned phone the school and make arrangements to see the most appropriate member of staff (see section 14). Neither the school nor the parent/carer should wait until parents' evening to bring up such worries. At these evenings there is only a limited time to talk with teachers about a child's progress and it can be in a fairly public space, like a school hall.

Ideally all contacts between school and home should be positive and friendly. It's in everybody's interests, especially the child's, to solve problems without slanging matches. A breakdown in relationships between school and home can have a devastating effect on a young person's attitude and progress.

16. PUPIL RECORDS.

If progress at school is to be properly monitored and tracked then it is essential that the recording and reporting processes used by schools are robust and easily transferable. Internal records relating to individual children are usually more than adequate but the sharing of that information across the school, with those who need to know, is not always as efficient as it might be, and the transferral of records between schools has traditionally been fraught with difficulties. Given the number of schools some children in care will attend during their school lives, it is relatively easy to imagine the problems that are likely to be encountered monitoring and tracking pupil performance, attendance and health or behavioural records. From 2010 all maintained secondary schools have been required to produce school reports electronically with primary schools following the same process from 2012.

> A common transfer form was introduced which has helped to reduce these problems. Now when children transfer between schools, maintained or independent, head teachers must send the completed statutory transfer form together with all educational records relating to the child, including copies of pupil reports. This must be sent within 15 days of the child being taken off the register at their former school. If the destination of the child is not known then school records should be transferred within 15 days of a request from a new school. This does not apply if:
>
> - The pupil has attended a school at which they have been registered for less than four weeks. In such circumstances it is assumed that records from a previous school will be forwarded
> - The most recent assessment information is not available. In this case the first half of the two-part form will be sent with further information to follow when available
> - The pupil is transferring to an institution of further or higher education. In such cases the transfer form should not be used and information is only transferred following a written request from the new placement.

All the manual and computerised personal information held by schools relating to your child is subject to the Data Protection Act.. This establishes:

- The right of parents, or those with parental responsibility, to see their children's records as long as the young person is under 18 years old
- The right of children to see their records, having submitted a written request, unless it is obvious they do not understand what they are asking for
- That nothing should be disclosed on children's records which would "be likely to cause serious harm to their physical or mental health or that of anyone else- including anything which suggests that they are, or have been, either the subject of, or at risk of, child abuse."

> This attempt to standardise the transferral of records between schools should result in receiving schools being in possession of much better quality information about their pupils, but there are always going to be difficulties when families and /or children re-locate on a frequent basis. In these cases persistence is absolutely essential. Further guidance relating to records or what data should be included/excluded is available from the Office of the Data Protection Commissioner. Address, telephone number and general advice can be found on the web site at **www.ico.gov.uk**

17. PARENT - TEACHER INTERVIEWS.

These generally fall into two categories:

1. Interviews that are arranged by parents or teachers in response to an issue or incidents that have occurred relating to school.
2. Scheduled meetings between parents and teachers, held at least once a year, to discuss your child's progress.

> In the first of these a meeting will have been requested by you or the teachers to discuss the progress, behaviour or well being of your child. Usually the meetings are held at a mutually convenient time on school premises, and in an area which allows a reasonable degree of privacy. Those organising the meeting should allow sufficient time for the issues to be aired by all sides, and any relevant documentation prepared before your arrival. The choice of who attends the meeting will very much depend on the nature of the problem to be discussed.
>
> In some cases the form tutor or class teacher might be the most appropriate member of staff to conduct the interview; in others a head teacher, deputy head or senior teacher could be in attendance. In many cases the young person will be present but there are times when it is beneficial to have at least part of the meeting without their presence.

If the meeting is to have a positive outcome it is vital that:

- All involved are well prepared and understand why they are there
- The meeting is conducted in a calm constructive atmosphere
- Everybody has an opportunity to put forward his or her point of view
- Proposals are made that are fair and signal a way forward
- Dates are set for reviewing of proposals or targets
- It is made absolutely clear what it is hoped will be achieved, who will monitor progress and what happens next.

It's always important to remind yourself why you are attending such meetings. It shouldn't be seen as a vehicle for settling old scores or generally attacking the school but as an opportunity to make life in school better and more productive for your child. Storming into school, as a small minority of parents are inclined to do, can not only be prejudicial to your case but can also cause severe embarrassment to your child. The more quickly schools react to incidents the less likely parents are to behave in an aggressive and contentious manner, but abusive or threatening behaviour is totally unacceptable. Court orders have been used to ban parents from school premises because of such behaviour, which is of little value to the child who is at the centre of the conflict.

Parents' evenings are very different types of meetings. These meetings are not always held in the evening, and are sometimes called review meetings or parent teacher interviews and they can be held at any time of the year. They are often timed to fit in with the annual report on a child's progress so that discussions with teachers can be based on recent observations and comments. If that is the case remember to take the report with you, it might be useful to make notes on. It is important that you attend because it sends such a strong message, first and foremost to your child, that you care what happens to them and are prepared to give them your full support.

Most schools have an appointment system for these interviews and they are often held in larger more public areas in schools, such as halls, libraries or classrooms. Time allocation can be as little as five minutes if the teacher has a lot of appointments, and there can be a great number of parents trying to move around the same area. It is, however, possible to make the meeting more than just an exercise you feel obliged to be part of, if you are organised and prepared to ask the right questions.

Getting the most out of parent – teacher interviews:

- Read any reports from the school before the interviews
- Decide if you want your child to accompany you, if there is an option
- Ask your child what sort of report they expect to receive from teachers and what questions they would like you to ask
- Make a note of the questions you would like to ask but remember to keep them brief
- Ensure appointments have been made with all staff you would like to see
- Take something to write brief notes on
- In a primary school you will probably see only one teacher but possibly between six and ten in a secondary school. If two carers attend they often decide to split up and speak with teachers separately
- Know the names of the teachers you are going to see, as well as the subjects they teach
- If the teacher says anything you don't understand, ask for clarification
- Ask what progress the young person has made
- Find out at what level they are working and how that compares with the rest of the group
- Ask about behaviour, attitude to work and relationships with other members of the group
- Be very wary about making comments relating to other students or members of staff
- Find out what support is needed from you
- Ask the teachers to follow up any areas of concern with a phone call to ascertain whether or not there has been any improvement.

It is possible that at the end of the interview you are disturbed by what you've heard and need to request a further meeting in school, as described in part 1 of this section, to ease your anxieties. Try not to take any action when you are angry or upset. Give yourself some time and space to think about what has been said. Parent-teacher interviews, in this context, are not the appropriate place to fully explore problems. Neither should you wait for these meetings before you tell the teachers about serious concerns. The school should be made aware of any serious issues as soon as they happen, especially if you need to speak in confidence to members of staff.

18. EXCLUSION.

The DFE produced figures in 2011 giving the latest statistics for school exclusions. These showed that approximately 900 children a day were excluded from state schools for violence or abuse. In total almost 300,000 children were excluded in the school year. Boys, Special Educational Needs pupils with statements and those on free school meals were much more likely to be excluded than other pupils.

If staff at a school feel they can no longer cope with the problems a child is causing then that child can be excluded from the school by a head or somebody acting in the head's place e.g. Deputy Head or senior teacher. If a decision is made to exclude it will either be a fixed term or permanent exclusion. Schools can also exclude pupils who are disruptive at lunch times. This would only be for the duration of lunch time. The excluded pupils will be able to attend lessons as normal apart from that. The school has to be able to show that great efforts have been made to change the behaviour of the excluded pupil but failed, or that allowing the child to remain in school would harm the welfare or education of other pupils. Most schools use a wide range of techniques to try and modify unacceptable behaviour. Such strategies are usually recorded in what are known as Pastoral Support Programmes (PSPs) and these should demonstrate what measures have been taken leading up to the exclusion. If the child in your care is excluded and you need help or support, ACE – The Advisory Centre for Education provides invaluable information. They can be contacted on: **0808 800 0327 or www.ace-ed.org.uk/advice.**

Exclusion should not be used for:
- Minor incidents such as failure to do homework
- Poor performance in lessons
- Lateness or truancy
- Pregnancy
- One-off uniform problems
- Punishing pupils for the behaviour of parents /carers

It is very important that you read the school handbook on discipline and codes of conduct so that you and your child understand what the school expects from its students and the consequences of not complying.

Since 2007 schools have been required to arrange full-time education for excluded pupils from the sixth day of exclusion.

The Government has also advised that Local Authorities should provide excluded secondary school pupils with 24/25 hours of teaching a week and excluded primary pupils with 21/23.5 hours depending on the key stage, just about what they would receive in school. However only a minority of LAs presently offer this and there are wide variations between authorities. Many schools are reluctant to admit or reintegrate excluded pupils and this has led to a backlog of students waiting for places at pupil referral units (see section 2). Since 2012 guidance from the DFE has suggested that head teachers have the right to refuse to re-admit students who have been permanently excluded. During 2012 a small number of authorities will trial a scheme where schools will be given funding to find alternative provision for permanently excluded pupils.

FIXED TERM EXCLUSIONS.

- Parents/carers should be told about ANY exclusion immediately, usually by phone, and then by letter within one school day giving the reason for the exclusion. The letter should also contain information about how to appeal against the exclusion and what arrangements will be made for the young person's return
- Pupils can be excluded for a total of 45 days in any school year
- The exclusion should be for the shortest possible time
- If it's for more than one day then school should set and mark work
- If it's for more than six days alternative suitable arrangements should be made for the pupil to receive full time education
- An appeal can be made against the exclusion by contacting the school governing body disciplinary committee.

PERMANENT EXCLUSIONS.

- This should only happen when everything else has failed but can also be used for a serious first time offence e.g. involving violence or drugs
- Again parents/carers should be informed immediately and written details of how to appeal, along with an LA contact, are likely to be in the letter you will receive about the exclusion
- It is now vital you work closely with any agency responsible for the child in your care
- The young person is still entitled to have work provided by the school until the governors confirm the exclusion
- A meeting will be arranged to discuss the case and you will be invited to give your views
- Even if a young person is permanently excluded it is the duty of the Local Authority to provide suitable, alternative education from the sixth day of exclusion
- The LA Education Officer MUST contact you to discuss what sort of education will be available for the young person in your care, after they have been permanently excluded
- Appropriate arrangements must be also be made for those students involved in examination courses.

Valuable guidance on exclusions can also be found at www.direct.gov.uk/en/parents.

19. EDUCATIONAL VISITS / SCHOOL TRIPS.

Educational activities beyond the classroom have always been, and hopefully will continue to be, an essential and exciting ingredient of a well-rounded education. It is often a time when really strong bonds and relationships develop not only between pupils but also between adult helpers and children. It is an opportunity to work as a team and socialise together in a far less formal setting than a classroom. Many teachers will admit that these are the occasions when they really get to know their students as individuals and no doubt most students would concede that it helped them to see another side to their teachers.

An educational visit is defined as "any excursion with children outside the perimeter of the school gates" (NAS/UWT advice to members) and at least one union has advised its teacher members not to take part in such visits. This is as a result of a number of rare but high profile cases where children have been seriously or even fatally injured during a trip or activity. Teachers have lost their jobs or gone to prison because of alleged errors of judgement, so it is not difficult to understand why they are nervous about taking on the responsibility of supervising groups of young people, especially when it involves an overnight stay. However in 2011 the Government responded to these concerns by producing helpful guidance and advice to ensure that such trips are not obstructed because of complex form filling. It will no longer be necessary to ask for parental consent to take part in off-site activities because the majority take place during the school day. Of course parents and carers must be informed of the activity so that they can withdraw their child if they have any concerns. Most schools are still involved in trips at home and abroad as well as involvement with museums, galleries, theatres, sporting occasions, camping, climbing and water sports, precisely because there is a belief amongst the staff that they are beneficial to the general development of all who take part, as well as being hugely enjoyable.

Of course you as carers are entitled to know what steps have been taken to ensure the safety of your child. Group leaders who are responsible for the health, safety and well being of the whole group must follow Government or Local Authority guidelines on educational visits. Leaders should have appropriate experience, qualifications and training and will have the duty of delegating tasks to other adult members of the group.

Leaders should also:

- Liaise with the head teacher or other senior members of staff responsible for visits and trips
- Assess the suitability of transport to and from the destination e.g. seat belts on coaches
- Carry out a pre-visit to assess the location for potential dangers and any problems that might be encountered travelling
- Ensure that accompanying adults are suitable and have been police checked
- Make suitable provision for insurance cover
- Have in place emergency procedures and contacts including medical arrangements
- Have a clear plan of activities
- Obtain the consent of parents or carers by communicating all arrangements, clearly detailing activities, codes of conduct, cost and timings etc.

> These are just a few of the arrangements that the leader will have put in place to facilitate the smooth running of a visit. It's not always appreciated how much effort goes into the organisation of one day visits off-site, let alone a trip abroad. For short trips, half a day or a whole day, letters are usually sent to parents giving information and asking for written permission. In the case of longer visits there is often a meeting at which you can ask more detailed questions about the itinerary, such as travelling or sleeping arrangements, general security and supervision of the pupils. The age of the young people in the group will determine issues such as how much freedom they will have, the amount of money they should carry and what time they will be expected to go to bed.

School trips and visits can offer children a huge variety of experiences away from parental supervision but in the care of responsible adults. Occasions like these are often treasured by those taking part for the rest of their lives. A well-organised visit, apart from the educational benefits, is an ideal way for young people to learn to socialise with other young people or adults and have a little of their own space, without having absolute freedom. Nobody can guarantee that there won't be incidents and accidents during some of these excursions, but thousands of educational visits take place every year without such traumas. Try to make your decision about a young person's involvement on the basis of an informed judgement about safety and supervisory arrangements, rather than the story of a tragic accident involving pupils from another school which may make headline news. Further information about health and safety provision for these visits can be found on the Department for Education (DFE) web site at **www.education.gov.uk**

20. CHILD EMPLOYMENT.

There is a great deal of discussion about this issue but much of it is dependent on the age of the young person, the type of work he or she is required to do and the length of the working day. Most people accept that given fairness in terms of pay and working conditions, and a safe environment in which to work, the experience can be extremely positive. It can have a beneficial effect on attitude, behaviour and social skills, which could potentially lead to improved performance in school or college.

It may be of particular value to those children who have not had the best life opportunities to prepare and develop for the world of work. Working in teams with other young people and adults can not only be a thoroughly enjoyable experience, but also highly motivational. Changes being made to the examination system and the curriculum generally should allow for greater vocational opportunities.

However employment can sometimes adversely impact on educational progress and that is where you might have to step in and make recommendations that may not always be welcomed by your child. They are not likely to see it as "for their own good" when they have been earning a bit of extra pocket money, even if the placement is unsuitable or, in extreme circumstances, dangerous.

The Protection of Young People Act 1998 was designed to protect young people from themselves and unscrupulous employers. The law stipulates that:

- The youngest age a child can work is 13 years. There are occasional exceptions, for assisting parents with light agricultural or horticultural work, and employment in theatre, film or television

- Employers must inform the LA when they are employing a child of school age. They are considered to be of school age up to the last Friday in the academic year of their 16th birthday

- Children must have a two-week break from any work during the school holidays, in any calendar year. They may work for a maximum of two hours on school days and on Sundays

- 13/14 year olds are allowed to work a maximum of 5 hours on Saturdays, and 15/16 year olds, 8 hours. The maximum working hours per week should not exceed twelve, except in school holidays, when 13/14 year olds are permitted to work up to 25 hours and 15/16 year olds 35 hours.

Children are not permitted to work:
- Without a Local Authority employment permit except when on school work experience
- In any industrial environment
- In occupations prohibited by local bye-laws e.g. pubs, betting shop
- For more than 1 hour before school
- More than 4 hours without a break of at least one hour
- During school hours
- Before 7am or after 7pm.

It must be remembered that these provisions are designed as protection for young people rather than a deterrent to employment whilst still at school. It also has to be accepted that some young people need protecting from themselves and the exploitation they frequently suffer at the hands of employers. The national minimum wage has applied to those over 18 for some years and from October 2004 it was extended to 16 and 17 year olds. From October 2011 national minimum wage rates were set at, £2.60 an hour - apprentice rate, £3.68 an hour for 16 and 17 year olds, £4.98 for 18-20 year olds and £6.08 for 21 and over. For further details see **www.direct.gov.uk/en/employment**

21. SOCIAL NETWORKING- SHOULD I BE WORRIED?

Well, you should certainly be aware of the uses and abuses of the technology available to the children in your care. It's fairly certain that most young people, especially adolescents, are very unlikely to share their online and mobile phone exploits with you. It is very difficult to ban or prevent them from using such networks. Recent research also shows that primary age children are increasingly involved in the use of such technology. Again this is difficult to avoid especially when an older brother or sister is accessing a variety of web sites. 70% of children under the age of ten now carry a mobile phone and the average age for owning a first phone is eight. There is no doubt that these advances have provided many beneficial effects. Communications are so much simpler and children can always make contact with somebody when they need help, or just to let you know they're going to be home late.

However with every innovation there is usually a downside and it is evident that thousands of young people experience the negative effects of social networking every year. Of course accessing inappropriate sites which may contain violent images or explicit sexual references are often the most disturbing to parents and carers but these may not be the most dangerous for your child and can at least be subjected to parental controls through your internet provider. What may be more worrying is who they are contacting, or being contacted by, either online through email, Facebook or Bebo etc, or through mobiles. Legitimate, well managed sites will have minimum age restrictions, usually 14, but that isn't a guarantee that younger people aren't communicating through them. Most young people have no problems with any of these new technologies. In the main they are immediate, mind expanding and great fun. It's not surprising then that the intervention of "paranoid oldies" into their amazing and often very secretive world is greeted with a fair amount of hostility. It may be that parents and carers become over protective and very concerned when they read or hear about a horrible incident linked with social networking, but they're not always wrong. The balance between protecting those in your care and interfering in their private lives is a very difficult one, but which parent hasn't worried about the information their child is revealing in online conversations? The innocent mention of a school, a birthday or an address can, through an unprotected profile, provide confidential information to a stranger whose intentions are not so innocent. A closed profile will help to ensure only those friends your child accepts on to the site can view any information.

WHAT TO LOOK OUT FOR

- Identity theft - This is more commonly associated with adults but should not be underestimated amongst young people. They should be advised never to reveal personal information.

- Cyber-bullying - A cowardly but sadly effective way of bullying from a distance and often anonymously. Offensive, abusive and malicious remarks are posted on line which can be extremely upsetting for the receiver. As with all bullying you must encourage your child to report any instances because comments posted have a nasty habit of attracting other copy-cat messages (see Sections 10, 14 and 17).

- On-line Grooming - Internet paedophiles have an unsavoury habit of searching chat rooms on social networking looking for a "friend." They will often pretend that they are of a similar age to the young person they are attempting to befriend. They will try to extract as much information as possible as a first step to manipulating them into doing what is asked of them, which can include lewd conversations and indecent images. They rely heavily on the fact that most young people will be too embarrassed to tell parents, other adults or even their friends what is happening.

Should you be at all concerned that the young person in your care has been approached in this way get help and advice immediately. You can report this sort of behaviour directly to the Child Exploitation and Online Protection Centre (CEOP) but if you think the child is in danger call 999.

Most parents and carers will have no need to resort to reporting matters of this kind to the police or any other agency, but it is better to be cautious and watchful about the use of technology by young people rather than assuming that they are sensible and old enough to make the right decisions.

USEFUL CONTACTS:

www.ceop.police.uk/Ceopreport
www.thinkuknow.co.uk/parents
www.childline.org.uk/ (Children who are anxious or distressed can call 0800 1111)
www.cybermentors.org.uk/ (Children can chat to young people of their own age about their problems)
www.netmums.com/yourchild (Very good advice from experienced parents and carers)

22. HOW TO COMPLAIN.

Surveys regularly demonstrate that the great majority of parents/carers are satisfied with the schools their children attend and the progress they make. It would be unusual, however, for parents not to be occasionally unhappy with situations that arise in schools. However, most incidents are fairly minor and can be dealt with promptly to the satisfaction of all parties, often through a brief telephone conversation. Others may require a meeting to allow a fuller airing of the issues with a resolution about how to move forward (see section 17) but it is important to remember that such meetings must be arranged in advance to ensure that the appropriate staff are able to attend.

When making a complaint:

- Make sure that you are in possession of accurate details
- Find out the names of those involved, teachers or students
- Find out, if possible, both sides of a story
- Resist dashing back into school for a confrontation. This can not only be embarrassing for your child but also potentially damaging to relationships between home and school
- Direct your complaint to the most appropriate member of staff (see section 14)
- Contact the school either in writing or by phone and ask for your complaint to be investigated
- Contact the head teacher or a senior member of staff if the matter is very serious or confidential
- Avoid making allegations unless you have evidence that they are true
- Make a brief note of any meeting attended or telephone calls exchanged, whom you were speaking with, and the outcome
- Try not to lose your temper. It is likely to result in the termination of a meeting.

Discussion and negotiation on a more informal level, with agreed continued monitoring of the situation, are the best ways to resolve many of the day-to-day problems in schools. Early intervention can often prevent the escalation of minor incidents into damaging conflicts between parents and teachers. It helps if you approach the school in a calm, reasonable manner with the intention of improving the situation for your child, not winning a personal battle. In those circumstances the school should be more than willing to listen to your anxieties as well as being sensitive to the needs of your child.

> Unfortunately not all complaints are resolved to the satisfaction of the parties involved and there are mechanisms in place for taking your concerns further. Since September 2003 governing bodies of all maintained schools and nursery schools have been obliged to have a complaints procedure in place. Copies should be readily available both to parents and carers as well as members of the general public. If you approach the governing body to formalise your complaint you should be aware that it might take some time for a response, because the members are unpaid volunteers and the chair of governors will need to contact them to arrange a meeting. It is, however, to be hoped that you will at least be kept informed of the progress being made to investigate your concerns.

If your child attends a maintained school there are two further avenues to explore if you feel that the governing body been unreasonable in responding to your complaint.

1. Approaching your Local Authority would be the next logical step to take. It will also have a complaints procedure to deal with issues not satisfactorily resolved at school level.
2. Should all else fail you have the right to take your complaint to the Secretary of State for Education at the DFE. This is an extreme measure and the vast majority of grievances are concluded well before this stage.

It should be noted that Academies and Free Schools (see Section 2) are no longer controlled by the Local Authorities. In that case parents would approach those schools first and if they are unhappy with the way the complaint is handled they would next contact the Education Funding Agency (EFA) at **academyquestions@efa.education.gov.uk.** If it involves an appeal about admissions or Special Needs see the DFE website.

Many of the complaints dealt with by LAs relate to school admissions (see Section 1). There is a legal right to appeal if you have been refused a place for your child in what is usually an oversubscribed school and an independent panel will be appointed to hear your appeal.

Other common grievances between home and school include:

- Homework
- Uniform policies
- Behaviour (Including bullying, racism and disruption of classes-see Section 10)
- Sanctions (Detention, working in isolation etc - see section 10)
- Setting or grouping arrangements (see section 5)
- Special needs (see section 12)
- Pupil absence from school – authorised or unauthorized (see Section 10)

Remember that most of these can be sorted out without recourse to lengthy complaints procedures, which carry a financial, and quite often an emotional cost.

23. TOP TWENTY TIPS FOR CARERS.

- Encourage the child in your care to be positive about school life and work.
- Defend the rights of the young person but support the school as much as possible.
- Make regular contact with teachers and support workers.
- Attend parents' evenings, reviews and meetings about the young person.
- Try and attend less formal occasions like plays, concerts, social evenings, exhibitions, fairs and sporting events.
- Be available.
- Work in partnership with school when trying to sort out problems.
- Inform school of any issues, which might affect progress or behaviour.
- Tell the school when you know in advance about an absence or as soon as possible on the day if it's unexpected.
- Don't make appointments in school time unless it's essential.
- As tempting as it is, avoid booking holidays in school time.
- Make sure all letters from school are dealt with promptly.
- Be aware when you need to escort young people to school. This may not always be age related; it might be to make sure they arrive!
- Be prepared to give time to them at the end of the school day by supporting learning tasks or just be available to listen to their views and opinions.
- Without being too obvious look for changes in mood or behaviour that might suggest problems in school.
- Be ready for the more stressful times in school e.g exams, problems with teachers or work, conflict with friends and other students. Work out tactics and ideas about how best to cope.
- Check homework and sign diaries or planners.
- Encourage the young person to use the local facilities for sport and leisure.
- Make sure there is plenty of access to reading and study materials.
- Encourage involvement in school activities outside school hours such as visits, outdoor activities, sports, drama, art or any other club that might interest the young person.

GLOSSARY OF TERMS.

One of the problems with teachers and many other professionals is that they develop their own language. This can become a bit of an obstacle to those trying to understand how to get the best out of the system for themselves or the young people they look after. Specialists in any field, doctors, plumbers, engineers and teachers, become so used to using particular terms and phrases that they forget that people outside those areas don't understand what they're talking about. We're often afraid to ask for an explanation because we don't want to appear ignorant or badly informed. Acronyms and abbreviations are widely used in education but not always explained. Below is a list of abbreviations, acronyms and terms or phrases that you are very likely to come across. Many will be found in sections of this handbook.

IN ALPHABETICAL ORDER.

A LEVEL	= advanced level (often called A2).
AS LEVEL	= advanced subsidiary level.
BSP	= behaviour support plan.
BTECs	= business and technology education council.
CRB	= criminal records bureau.
CTCs	= city technology colleges.
DFE	= the department for education
EBD	= emotional and behavioural difficulties.
EWO	= educational welfare officer.
EWS	= education welfare service.
FSW	= family support worker.
GCSE	= general certificate of secondary education.
G&T	= gifted and talented.
GNVQ	= general national vocational qualification.
HOD	= head of department.
HOY	= head of year.
ICT	= information and communication technology.
IEP	= individual education plan.
KS	= key stage.
LAC	= looked after children.
LASW	= local authority social worker..
LA	= local authority.
LSA	= learning support assistant.
MFL	= modern foreign languages.
MLD	= mild learning difficulties.
NC	= national curriculum.
NTA	= non-teaching assistant.
NVQ	= national vocational qualification.
NQT	= newly qualified teacher.
Ofsted	= office for standards in education.
PSP	= pastoral support programme.
PEP	= personal education plan.
PMLD	= profound and multiple learning difficulties.
PRU	= pupil referral unit.
QCA	= qualifications and curriculum authority.
PTA	= parent teacher association.
SATs	= standard assessment tests.
SEN	= special educational needs.
SENCO	= special educational needs co-ordinator.
SLD	= severe learning difficulties.
SpLD	= specific learning difficulties.
UCAS	= university and college admissions service.